Instant Play Framework Starter

Build your web applications from the ground up with the Play Framework for Java and Scala

Daniel Dietrich

BIRMINGHAM - MUMBAI

Instant Play Framework Starter

Copyright © 2013 Packt Publishing

All rights reserved. No part of this book may be reproduced, stored in a retrieval system, or transmitted in any form or by any means, without the prior written permission of the publisher, except in the case of brief quotations embedded in critical articles or reviews.

Every effort has been made in the preparation of this book to ensure the accuracy of the information presented. However, the information contained in this book is sold without warranty, either express or implied. Neither the author, nor Packt Publishing, and its dealers and distributors will be held liable for any damages caused or alleged to be caused directly or indirectly by this book.

Packt Publishing has endeavored to provide trademark information about all of the companies and products mentioned in this book by the appropriate use of capitals. However, Packt Publishing cannot guarantee the accuracy of this information.

First published: May 2013

Production Reference: 1170513

Published by Packt Publishing Ltd.
Livery Place
35 Livery Street
Birmingham B3 2PB, UK.

ISBN 978-1-78216-290-2

www.packtpub.com

Credits

Author
Daniel Dietrich

Reviewers
Takafumi Ikeda
Jérôme Leleu

Acquisition Editor
James Jones

Commissioning Editor
Sharvari Tawde

Technical Editors
Sharvari Baet
Chirag Jani
Soumya Kanti

Project Coordinator
Suraj Bist

Proofreader
Paul Hindle

Production Coordinator
Aparna Bhagat

Cover Work
Aparna Bhagat

Cover Image
Valentina Dsilva

About the Author

Daniel Dietrich is a Senior Software Engineer living in Kiel, Germany. He studied Computer Science with Mathematics as a subsidiary subject and earned his diploma degree at the Christian-Albrechts University of Kiel. He specializes in enterprise grade frontend and backend development with a current focus on building a financial risk services platform.

Daniel has been developing software for over 25 years, thereof, 15 years professionally. He started to program at the age of 11. His creative work was influenced by computer competitions during the 90s. In the late 90s, he began to develop web applications.

Daniel worked as a Software Developer for several companies and is currently employed at the HSH Nordbank. He is focused on designing enterprise architectures and implementing Java enterprise applications. He has a special interest in JVM languages and web frameworks, especially Scala and the Play Framework.

> I want to thank my beloved wife Andrea—I am deeply thankful for her support and her unconditional devotion.
>
> I also want to thank my wonderful kids, Emil, Leni, and Paul for being so patient when daddy sits in front of his notebook.
>
> A special thanks goes to Ingo Hammer for supporting me at the HSH Nordbank.
>
> My last appreciation goes to everyone at Packt Publishing who was involved in this project, especially Poonam Jain, Meeta Rajani, Sharvari Tawde, and Suraj Bist.

About the Reviewers

Takafumi Ikeda is the maintainer of Play Framework 1 and currently works as the Developer Advocate of a mobile gaming platform. He is also the author of the Jenkins Play Framework plugin and is also the representative of Japanense Play Framework users group. He has written several articles about Play on Japan tech media and has also talked about technical matters, especially about Play, in tech conferences/seminars in Japan. You can contact him on Twitter `@ikeike443` (in Japanese) or `@Takafumi_Ikeda` (in English).

Jérôme Leleu is a Software Architect living in Paris, France.

A Consultant for 7 years, he has worked in many different companies, fields, and with many different people. He has participated in many IT projects as a Developer, Technical Lead, or Projects Manager, mostly with J2EE technology.

Now working in a French telecom company, he is the Software Architect of the company's web SSO, which supports very high traffic: millions of authentications from millions of users every day. He's also leading the software architecture of the company website.

He is involved in open source development as a CAS (web SSO) Committer. Interested in security/protocol issues, he has developed several libraries, one of which is a Java and Scala client for the Play 2 Framework to protect an application with CAS, OAuth, OpenID, or HTTP protocols.

www.packtpub.com

Support files, eBooks, discount offers and more

You might want to visit `www.packtpub.com` for support files and downloads related to your book.

Did you know that Packt offers eBook versions of every book published, with PDF and ePub files available? You can upgrade to the eBook version at `www.packtpub.com` and as a print book customer, you are entitled to a discount on the eBook copy. Get in touch with us at `service@packtpub.com` for more details.

At `www.packtpub.com`, you can also read a collection of free technical articles, sign up for a range of free newsletters and receive exclusive discounts and offers on Packt books and eBooks.

packtlib.packtpub.com

Do you need instant solutions to your IT questions? PacktLib is Packt's online digital book library. Here, you can access, read and search across Packt's entire library of books.

Why Subscribe?

- ✦ Fully searchable across every book published by Packt
- ✦ Copy and paste, print and bookmark content
- ✦ On demand and accessible via web browser

Free Access for Packt account holders

If you have an account with Packt at www.packtpub.com, you can use this to access PacktLib today and view nine entirely free books. Simply use your login credentials for immediate access.

Table of Contents

Instant Play Framework Starter — 1
So, what is Play? — 3
Installation — 4
- Step 1 – What do I need? — 4
- Step 2 – Downloading Play — 4
- Step 3 – Setting the PATH environment variable — 5
- Step 4 – Testing the Play installation — 6
- And that's it! — 6

Quick start – Creating your first Play application — 7
- Step 1 – Creating a new Play application — 7
  - Structure of a Play application — 8
- Step 2 – Using the Play console — 10
  - Starting our application — 10
  - Play console commands — 11
  - Closing the console — 11
- Step 3 – Modifying our application — 12
  - Fast turnaround – change your code and hit reload! — 12
  - Stripped down and optimized stack traces — 13
- Step 4 – Setting up your preferred IDE — 13
  - IntelliJ IDEA — 14
  - Eclipse — 14
  - Other IDEs — 15

Top features you need to know about — 16
- 1 – Designing a Play application — 16
  - Introducing our sample application — 16
  - Defining the domain model — 16
  - Designing the HTTP interface with the routes file — 19
  - Handling HTTP requests by controller actions — 21
  - Composing the UI from view templates — 26
  - Implementing the phone book views — 28

Table of Contents

2 – Dealing with user input	33
Defining a form	33
Validating user input	37
Using form template helpers	41
3 – Connecting to a database	42
Accessing data with Ebean for Java	43
Accessing data with Anorm for Scala	47
Accessing data with Slick for Scala	50
People and places you should get to know	**54**
Official sites	54
Articles and tutorials	54
Community	54
Blogs	55
Twitter	55
About Packt Publishing	57
Writing for Packt	57

Instant Play Framework Starter

Welcome to *Instant Play Framework Starter*. This book has been especially created to provide you with all the information that you need to get started with the Play Framework for Java and Scala. You will learn the basics of Play, get involved with building your first application, and discover some tips and tricks for using Play.

This book contains the following sections:

So, what is Play? will give you a brief overview of the functionality of the Play Framework. Find out why Play is actually the best choice for creating a new web application with Java or Scala.

Installation will teach you how to get the Play Framework up and running so that you can use it as soon as possible. After downloading and installing Play, you will set it up with the minimum fuss.

Quick start – Creating your first Play application will provide you with the knowledge needed to perform one of the core tasks of Play; creating applications. In a few steps, you will easily create your first Java or Scala application and start it in a web browser.

Top features you need to know about will teach you how to develop dynamic web applications with Play for Java and Scala. By the end of this section, you will be able to design scalable web applications, exchange and validate data in a type-safe way, and persist it to a database.

People and places you should get to know provides you with many useful links to the project page and forums, as well as a number of helpful articles, tutorials, blogs, and the Twitter feeds of Play super-contributors.

So, what is Play?

Play is a full-stack web framework created to make web application development on the JVM easier and more productive. It provides APIs for Java and Scala.

A full-stack web framework provides solutions for a wide range of time-consuming web development tasks. With Play, developers are focusing on implementing functionality instead of thinking about design and architecture, and re-inventing the wheel. Only a few lines are necessary to write a fully functional web application.

Traditional web frameworks running on the JVM tend to create an abstraction layer over another abstraction layer. These heavy-weight lasagne architectures introduce an additional technical boilerplate and configuration, distracting developers from reaching their goal. Play in turn reduces complexity and simplifies web development by aligning its architecture with the that of the web, instead of abstracting it away.

Users of the Play Framework are web developers. Developers care about code readability and maintainability, fast development cycles, and easy error recovery. Play was designed by web developers to meet these goals.

Play consists of well-known parts. The basic architecture of a Play application follows the model-view-controller pattern, having an HTTP interface at its heart. Cohesive controllers and composable views share the same model.

Code changes are made visible by a simple reload of the web page in the browser. Play takes care of compiling changes in the background, independent of the development environment. This makes the development turnaround fast and easy.

Play also takes care of errors. Developers don't have to read long JVM stack traces to locate an error. Instead, Play shows the significant information directly in the browser, leading the developer right to the origin of the error. It is a big advantage that Play is a JVM framework; almost all parts of a Play application are type-safe.

This is why it is fun to develop Play applications.

Installation

In four easy steps, we can install Play and get it set up on our system.

Step 1 – What do I need?

Before you install Play, you need to check if JDK 6 or later is installed, which can be downloaded here: `http://www.oracle.com/technetwork/java/javase/downloads`

> The JDK should be pre-installed on Mac OS X and Linux. The OpenJDK, a viable open-source alternative to the Oracle JDK, is already a part of many Linux distributions. Windows users should download and install the latest JDK as mentioned previously.

This is the only requirement. Play is bundled with its own web server and build environment, so we don't have to install additional software.

As mentioned previously, Play provides more than just an API for programming web applications—Play is a full-stack web framework that also takes care of building and running your application. You can use your preferred editor or IDE to develop a Play application. Modifications to your source code are automatically detected and the running application is refreshed by Play.

Step 2 – Downloading Play

The easiest way to download Play is as a compressed package from `http://www.playframework.org/download`.

> For Mac users with Homebrew installed, it's even easier to install Play. The command `brew install play` will install the latest version of Play and set the `PATH` environment variable accordingly. For managing multiple versions of Play, it is definitely worth taking a look at `https://github.com/kaiinkinen/pvm`.

We suggest that you download the most current stable build. After downloading, the archive has to be unpacked to a place where you have read and write permissions. This is necessary because Play caches all library dependencies in a file system repository. After unpacking the archive, you will be left with a directory called `play-2.1` or similar, depending on the downloaded version. The extracted directory contains a number of files and folders.

```
/path/to/play
    | CONTRIBUTING.md     instructions for committing code
```

```
| README.md          basic instructions on using Play
| play               Mac/Linux start script
| play.bat           Windows start script
└─documentation      manual and API specification
└─framework          Play project files and sources
└─repository         downloaded dependencies
└─samples            sample application for Java and Scala
```

Here you find the Play start scripts `play` for Mac/Linux and `play.bat` for Windows. The `documentation` folder contains the user manual and the API specification, which will accompany you when developing an application. In the `samples` folder, you will find the source code of the examples shipped with Play. They are a great learning resource when you have understood the basics of Play and want to go further, so take a look at them. Both the documentation and the samples are available for Java and Scala developers.

The remaining folders are of less interest to us in this book; `framework` contains the Play project files and sources and `repository` contains additional downloaded libraries and dependencies.

Step 3 – Setting the PATH environment variable

Before creating our first Play application, we have to ensure that the Play installation directory is added to the system path. This makes it possible to start Play from the console without specifying the complete path of the `start` script.

Please open a text editor of your choice. Depending on the underlying OS, the PATH environment variable is set up as follows:

+ **Mac OS**: To set up the PATH environment variable, add the line `export PATH=$PATH:/path/to/play` to the file `~/.bash_profile`, where `/path/to/play` points to the location where you have installed Play.

+ **Linux**: To set up the PATH environment variable, add the line `export PATH=$PATH:/path/to/play` to your shell configuration file, for example, add the line to `~/.bashrc` if you use the bash shell. Again, `/path/to/play` points to the Play installation directory.

+ **Windows**: To permanently add Play to your environment settings, open a terminal window and execute the following command: `setx PATH "%PATH%;c:\path\to\play" -m`. Please change the path `c:\path\to\play` according to the path of your Play installation directory.

Instant Play Framework Starter

Step 4 – Testing the Play installation

Now we are ready to start Play. Test your installation by opening a new command-line window. Then type the `play` command. The Play script should produce output on the screen similar to this:

```
$ play
      _            _
 _ __ | | __ _ _  _| |
| '_ \| |/ _` | || |_|
|  __/|_|\__,_|\_, (_)
|_|            |__/

play! 2.1.0 (using Java 1.6.0_37 and Scala 2.10.0), http://www.playframework.org

This is not a play application!

Use `play new` to create a new Play application in the current directory,
or go to an existing application and launch the development console using `play`.

You can also browse the complete documentation at http://www.playframework.org.

$
```

The output of the `play` script shows us the error message **This is not a play application!**. You will see that it is characteristic for Play to provide hints for fixing errors. In this case Play gives us two options:

- Use `play new` to create a new Play application in the current directory
- Go to an existing application and launch the development console using `play`

We will discuss both topics in the next section.

And that's it!

Congratulations, by this point, you should have a working installation of Play and are free to play around and discover more about it.

Instant Play Framework Starter

Quick start – Creating your first Play application

Now that we have a working Play installation in place, we will see how easy it is to create and run a new application with just a few keystrokes.

Besides walking through the structure of our Play application, we will also look at what we can do with the command-line interface of Play and how fast modifications of our application are made visible.

Finally, we will take a look at the setup of **integrated development environments** (**IDEs**).

Step 1 – Creating a new Play application

So, let's create our first Play application. In fact, we create two applications, because Play comes with the APIs for Java and Scala, the sample accompanying us in this book is implemented twice, each in one separate language.

[Please note that it is generally possible to use both languages in one project.]

Following the DRY principle, we will show code only once if it is the same for the Java and the Scala application. In such cases we will use the play-starter-scala project.

First, we create the Java application. Open a command line and change to a directory where you want to place the project contents. Run the `play` script with the `new` command followed by the application name (which is used as the directory name for our project):

```
$ play new play-starter-java
```

We are asked to provide two additional information:

- The application name, for display purposes. Just press the *Enter* key here to use the same name we passed to the `play` script. You can change the name later by editing the `appName` variable in `play-starter-java/project/Build.scala`.
- The template we want to use for the application. Here we choose **2** for Java.

Repeat these steps for our Scala application, but now choose **1** for the Scala template. Please note the difference in the application name:

```
$ play new play-starter-scala
```

Instant Play Framework Starter

The following screenshot shows the output of the `play new` command:

```
$ play new play-starter-scala
       _            _
 _ __ | | __ _ _  _| |
| '_ \| |/ _' | || |_|
|  __/|_|\__,_|\_ (_)
|_|            |__/

play! 2.1.0 (using Java 1.6.0_37 and Scala 2.10.0), http://www.playframework.org

The new application will be created in /path/to/play-starter-scala

What is the application name? [play-starter-scala]
>

Which template do you want to use for this new application?

  1             - Create a simple Scala application
  2             - Create a simple Java application

> 1
OK, application play-starter-scala is created.

Have fun!

$
```

On our way through the next sections, we will build an ongoing example step-by-step. We will see Java and Scala code side-by-side, so create both projects if you want to find out more about the difference between Java and Scala based Play applications.

Structure of a Play application

Physically, a Play application consists of a series of folders containing source code, configuration files, and web page resources. The `play new` command creates the standardized directory structure for these files:

```
/path/to/play-starter-scala
    └app                    source code
    | └controllers          http request processors
    | └views                templates for html files
    └conf                   configuration files
    └project                sbt project definition
    └public                 folder containing static assets
    | └images               images
    | └javascripts          javascript files
    | └stylesheets          css style sheets
    └test                   source code of test cases
```

During development, Play generates several other directories, which can be ignored, especially when using a version control system:

```
/path/to/play-starter-scala
    └─dist               releases in .zip format
    └─logs               log files
    └─project            THIS FOLDER IS NEEDED
    |   └─project        but this...
    |   └─target         ...and this can be ignored
    └─target             generated sources and binaries
```

There are more folders that can be found in a Play application depending on the IDE we use. In particular, a Play project has optional folders on more involved topics we do not discuss in this book. Please refer to the Play documentation for more details.

The app/ folder

The `app/` folder contains the source code of our application. According to the MVC architectural pattern, we have three separate components in the form of the following directories:

- `app/models/`: This directory is not generated by default, but it is very likely present in a Play application. It contains the business logic of the application, for example, querying or calculating data.
- `app/views/`: In this directory we find the view templates. Play's view templates are basically HTML files with dynamic parts.
- `app/controllers/`: This controllers contain the application specific logic, for example, processing HTTP requests and error handling.

The default directory (or package) names, `models`, `views`, and `controllers`, can be changed if needed.

The conf/ directory

The `conf/` directory is the place where the application's configuration files are placed. There are two main configuration files:

- `application.conf`: This file contains standard configuration parameters
- `routes` – This file defines the HTTP interface of the application

The `application.conf` file is the best place to add more configuration options if needed for our application.

Configuration files for third-party libraries should also be put in the `conf/` directory or an appropriate sub-directory of `conf/`.

Instant Play Framework Starter

The project/ folder

Play builds applications with the **Simple Build Tool** (**SBT**). The `project/` folder contains the SBT build definitions:

- `Build.scala`: This is the application's build script executed by SBT
- `build.properties`: This definition contains properties such as the SBT version
- `plugins.sbt`: This definition contains the SBT plugins used by the project

The public/ folder

Static web resources are placed in the `public/` folder. Play offers standard sub-directories for images, CSS stylesheets, and JavaScript files. Use these directories to keep your Play applications consistent.

Create additional sub-directories of `public/` for third-party libraries for a clear resource management and to avoid file name clashes.

The test/ folder

Finally, the `test/` folder contains unit tests or functional tests. This code is not distributed with a release of our application.

Step 2 – Using the Play console

Play provides a command-line interface (CLI), the so-called Play console. It is based on the SBT and provides several commands to manage our application's development cycle.

Starting our application

To enter the Play console, open a shell, change to the root directory of one of our Play projects, and run the `play` script.

```
$ cd /path/to/play-starter-scala
$ play
```

On the Play console, type `run` to run our application in **development** (**DEV**) mode.

```
[play-starter-scala] $ run
```

> Use `~run` instead of `run` to enable automatic compilation of file changes. This gives us an additional performance boost when accessing our application during development and it is recommended by the author.
>
> All console commands can be called directly on the command line by running `play <command>`. Multiple arguments have to be denoted in quotation marks, for example, `play "~run 9001"`.

A web server is started by Play, which will listen for HTTP requests on `localhost:9000` by default. Now open a web browser and go to this location.

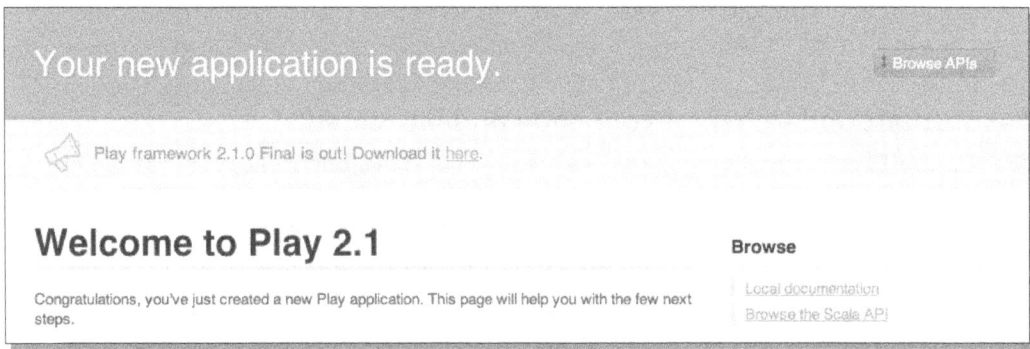

The page displayed by the web browser is the default implementation of a new Play application.

To return to our shell, type the keys *Ctrl + D* to stop the web server and get back to the Play console.

Play console commands

Besides `run`, we typically use the following console commands during development:

- `clean`: This command deletes cached files, generated sources, and compiled classes
- `compile`: This command compiles the current application
- `test`: This command executes unit tests and functional tests

We get a list of available commands by typing `help play` in the Play development console.

A release of an application is started with the `start` command in **production** (**PROD**) mode. In contrast to the DEV mode no internal state is displayed in the case of an error.

There are also commands of the `play` script, available only on the command line:

- `clean-all`: This command deletes all generated directories, including the logs.
- `debug`: This command runs the Play console in debug mode, listening on the JPDA port 9999. Setting the environment variable `JDPA_PORT` changes the port.
- `stop`: This command stops an application that is running in production mode.

Closing the console

We exit the Play console and get back to the command line with the `exit` command or by simply typing the key *Ctrl + D*.

Instant Play Framework Starter

Step 3 – Modifying our application

We now come to the part that we love the most as impatient developers: the rapid development turnaround cycles. In the following sections, we will make some changes to the given code of our new application visible.

Fast turnaround – change your code and hit reload!

First we have to ensure that our applications are running. In the root of each of our Java and Scala projects, we start the Play console. We start our Play applications in parallel on two different ports to compare them side-by-side with the commands `~run` and `~run 9001`. We go to the browser and load both locations, `localhost:9000` and `localhost:9001`.

Then we open the default controller `app/controllers/Application.java` and `app/controllers/Application.scala` respectively, which we created at application creation, in a text editor of our choice, and change the message to be displayed in the Java code:

```java
public class Application extends Controller {
    public static Result index() {
        return ok(index.render("Look ma! No restart!"));
    }
}
```

and then in the Scala code:

```scala
object Application extends Controller {
  def index = Action {
    Ok(views.html.index("Look ma! No restart!"))
  }
}
```

Finally, we reload our web pages and immediately see the changes:

That's it. We don't have to restart our server or re-deploy our application. The code changes take effect by simply reloading the page.

Stripped down and optimized stack traces

If we make a change to our application that does not compile and refresh the browser, Play shows us exactly where the error is. Also, it provides us with a single message that tells us the cause of the compile error.

An example is shown as follows (only the Java code is shown here, feel free to play around):

```
public class Application extends Controller {

    public static Result index() {
        return "Look ma! No restart!";
    }

}
```

The previous change does not compile, and it leads to the following error:

```
Compilation error

incompatible types [found: java.lang.String] [required: play.mvc.Result]
In /path/to/play-starter-java/app/controllers/Application.java at line 11.

 8  public class Application extends Controller {
 9
10      public static Result index() {
11          return "Look ma! No restart!";
12      }
13
14  }
```

Please note that these error messages are only shown in development mode. There are no internals exposed to the users when running in production mode.

Step 4 – Setting up your preferred IDE

Play takes care of automatically compiling modifications we make to our source code. That is why we don't need a full-blown IDE to develop Play applications. We can use a simple text editor instead.

However, using an IDE has many advantages, such as code completion, refactoring assistance, and debugging capabilities. Also it is very easy to navigate through the code. Therefore, Play has built-in project generation support for two of the most popular IDEs: **IntelliJ IDEA** and **Eclipse**.

Instant Play Framework Starter

IntelliJ IDEA

The free edition, *IntelliJ IDEA Community*, can be used to develop Play projects. However, the commercial release, *IntelliJ IDEA Ultimate*, includes Play 2.0 support for Java and Scala. Currently, it offers the most sophisticated features compared to other IDEs.

More information can be found here: `http://www.jetbrains.com/idea` and also here: `http://confluence.jetbrains.com/display/IntelliJIDEA/Play+Framework+2.0`

We generate the required IntelliJ IDEA project files by typing the `idea` command on the Play console or by running it on the command line:

```
$ play idea
```

We can also download the available source JAR files by running `idea with-source=true` on the console or on the command line:

```
$ play "idea with-source=true"
```

After that, the project can be imported into IntelliJ IDEA. Make sure you have the IDE plugins *Scala*, *SBT*, and *Play 2* (if available) installed.

The project files have to be regenerated by running `play idea` every time the classpath changes, for example, when adding or changing project dependencies. IntelliJ IDEA will recognize the changes and reloads the project automatically. The generated files should not be checked into a version control system, as they are specific to the current environment.

Eclipse

Eclipse is also supported by Play. The *Eclipse Classic* edition is fine, which can be downloaded here: `http://www.eclipse.org/downloads`.

It is recommended to install the *Scala IDE* plugin, which comes up with great features for Scala developers and can be downloaded here: `http://scala-ide.org`. You need to download Version 2.1.0 (milestone) or higher to get Scala 2.10 support for Play 2.1.

> A Play 2 plugin exists also for Eclipse, but it is in a very early stage. It will be available in a future release of the Scala IDE. More information can be found here: `https://github.com/scala-ide/scala-ide-play2/wiki`

The best way to edit Play templates with Eclipse currently is by associating HTML files with the *Scala Script Editor*. You get this editor by installing the *Scala Worksheet* plugin, which is bundled with the Scala IDE.

We generate the required Eclipse project files by typing the `eclipse` command on the Play console or by running it on the command line:

```
$ play eclipse
```

Analogous to the previous code, we can also download available source JAR files by running `eclipse with-source=true` on the console or on the command line:

```
$ play "eclipse with-source=true"
```

Also, don't check in generated project files for a version control system or regenerate project files if dependencies change. Eclipse (Juno) is recognizing the changed project files automatically.

Other IDEs

Other IDEs are not supported by Play out of the box. There are a couple of plugins, which can be configured manually. For more information on this topic, please consult the Play documentation.

Top features you need to know about

We will develop a sample application in Java and Scala, which will accompany us throughout this book. First, we will take a close look at the anatomy of a Play application. Then we will deal with user input. Finally, we will explore the different ways to talk to a database with Play.

1 – Designing a Play application

In this section we will learn the basics of how to implement the MVC components of a typical Play application.

Introducing our sample application

Our sample here is a prototype of a phone book application. We are maintaining our contacts with it, where the contacts have a name and a phone number. We are able to add, remove, and edit contacts. Additionally, we will implement a search for contacts.

All source code needed to run the example is found in this book. However, it is also available online at `http://packtpub.com` and `http://bit.ly/PhoneBookSample` for each step that we perform.

Defining the domain model

We already know that a Play application follows the MVC architectural pattern. It is up to us which component we implement first. We decide to start implementing the model. The model reflects the business requirements, in that it contains the business logic and our entities.

First of all, we have to ensure our applications are started in development mode with the `~run` command, as described previously.

The Java model

We create the package `models` in the `app/` folder of our Java application and add a new entity class `Entry.java` to it. As mentioned before, the package name `models` can be changed if needed.

```
package models;

public class Entry {

  public Long id;
  public String name;
  public String phone;

}
```

The `Entry` class represents phone book entries. Objects of this class contain a specific `name` and `phone` entity. Also we need a unique identifier, `id`, to be able to distinguish phone book entries. Especially, it is allowed to create multiple entries with the same name and phone number. Please note that phone numbers are of type `String`, because we also want to allow characters other than digits.

For the sake of simplicity, the visibility of the properties is `public` to omit the implementation of getters and setters.

Next, we need to create our **data access object** (**DAO**). We choose to name it `Entries.java`. To keep it simple, we place it in the same package:

```java
package models;

import static play.libs.Scala.toSeq;

import java.util.*;
import java.util.concurrent.ConcurrentHashMap;
import java.util.concurrent.atomic.AtomicLong;

import scala.collection.Seq;

public class Entries {

  private static Map<Long, Entry> entries =
      new ConcurrentHashMap<Long, Entry>();

  private static AtomicLong uuid = new AtomicLong();

  public static void delete(long id) {
    entries.remove(id);
  }

  public static Entry findById(long id) {
    return entries.get(id);
  }

  public static Seq<Entry> findByName(String filter) {
    List<Entry> result = new ArrayList<Entry>();
    for (Entry entry : entries.values()) {
      if (entry.name.toLowerCase()
          .contains(filter.toLowerCase())) {
        result.add(entry);
      }
    }
```

Instant Play Framework Starter

```
      return toSeq(result);
    }

    public static void save(Entry entry) {
      if (entry.id == null) {
        entry.id = uuid.incrementAndGet();
      }
      entries.put(entry.id, entry);
    }

  }
```

The DAO consists of static methods only and we will not create instances of that class. This *pattern* is also found in controllers and reflects a fundamental idea of the Play framework; to encourage us to follow a stateless programming model.

Phone book entries can be deleted by an `entry id` entity. We search entries by their ID and by their name. The `findByName` implementation returns a list of entries (of type `Seq`) that contain a specific string in their name, ignoring the case. If the search string is empty, all entries are returned. The order of list items is undetermined here.

 We use the Scala collection type `Seq` here because it is shared by the views of our Java and Scala examples. Java developers typically use `List` instead.

Finally, the entries can be saved. The `save` method equips new entries with an ID. Existing entries are updated in the underlying storage. Our storage is a map associating IDs with the corresponding entries.

The Scala model

Our Scala implementation of the model resides in `app/models/` in the file `Entries.scala`:

```
package models

import scala.collection.concurrent.TrieMap
import java.util.concurrent.atomic.AtomicLong

case class Entry(name: String = "", phone: String = "",
    id: Option[Long] = None)

object Entries {

  val entries = TrieMap[Long, Entry]()
```

```scala
    val uuid: AtomicLong = new AtomicLong()
    def delete(id: Long) = entries.remove(id)
    def findById(id: Long) = entries.get(id)
    def findByName(filter: String) = entries.values.filter {
      _.name.toLowerCase.contains(filter.toLowerCase)
    }.toSeq
    def save(entry: Entry) =
      ( if (entry.id.isDefined) entry
        else entry.copy(id = Some(uuid.incrementAndGet()))
      ) match {
        case e@Entry(_, _, Some(id)) => entries += (id -> e)
      }
  }
```

This contains both the `entry` entity and the `entries` DAO. `Entry` is a *case class*, which allows us to implement data beans in a very concise way, literally as a one-liner.

The functionality of our Java and Scala DAO implementations is the same here. The entity is containing the data and will be part of our interface between view and controller. Only the controller is permitted to use the DAO to access the data layer.

Designing the HTTP interface with the routes file

HTTP requests and responses are first-class citizens of Play. The HTTP interface forms the core of a Play application. It is defined in the `conf/routes` file and contains a mapping of HTTP requests to the corresponding method calls. An entry of this file is called *route* and looks like this:

```
GET      /                         controllers.Application.index
```

In particular, the left-hand side of the route consists of two parts: the *HTTP method* and the *request path*, which is relative to the base URL of the application.

Here, the `Application.index` method is called when we open a browser and visit the base URL, that is, the request path /, of our application. Such a request is sent with the `GET` method.

Valid methods are `GET`, `POST`, `PUT`, `DELETE`, `OPTIONS`, `HEAD`, and `WS`.

Defining the application routes

In our example the `GET` and `POST` methods are sufficient. Described in a nutshell, we use the `GET` method to load a specific web page without modifying a resource and the `POST` method to change a resource and navigate to a result page.

Instant Play Framework Starter

Please insert the following code lines behind the first route definition of the `conf/routes` file of both the projects (Java and Scala):

```
GET     /entries                controllers.Entries.list(filter ?= "")
GET     /entries/new            controllers.Entries.add
GET     /entries/:id            controllers.Entries.edit(id: Long)
POST    /entries/:id/remove     controllers.Entries.remove(id: Long)
POST    /entries                controllers.Entries.save
```

Routes are processed in the order of their occurrence until a match is found. If no route matches the actual URL, Play returns a **HTTP 404 Not Found** page.

The first line reflects that we want to retrieve a *list* of phone book entries filtered by a specific search string. We are planning to add controls to the phone book list that will allow us to *add* new phone book entries, *edit* existing ones, and *remove* entries.

If we add or edit an entry, we navigate to a phone book entry details page. After the user has finished editing the entry on the client side, it can be *saved* or *canceled*. In both cases, we want to return back to the entry list page.

Dynamic request paths and variables

There is one thing we have not explained yet regarding our new routes. Play allows a special notation of the request path of the route. There are three kinds of placeholders for path segments we can use:

- `$name<regex>`: The dollar sign $ marks a placeholder for the match of a regular expression `regex`. The current value can be accessed by `name`. The path segments are processed case sensitive.
- `:name`: The colon : matches exactly one request path segment. It is internally mapped to the regular expression `$name<[^/]+>`.
- `*name`: The asterisk * matches the remaining path segments and can be used to express whole paths. It is internally mapped to the regular expression `$name<.+>`.

The first two placeholders can be combined in a request path, such as:

```
/shop/:product/$number<[0-9]+>/details
```

Given that, `/shop/socks/1234/details` is a valid request path, where `product` is `socks` and `number` is `1234`. We pass these placeholders to a controller method, say:

```
controllers.Shop.showProductDetails(product: String, number: Int)
```

Also, please note that Play takes care of converting the text content of the extracted path segments to the appropriate parameter types declared in the controller method. The trailing parentheses are optional if the controller method has no arguments.

If we declare a controller method parameter that has no corresponding request path placeholder, Play tries to find that value in the HTTP request header. In other words, the parameter can be specified as a URL query string parameter `shop?product=socks`.

Additionally, we can define a special handling for controller method parameters:

- `product: String = "socks"`: This defines the *fixed* value `socks`
- `product: String ?= "socks"`: This defines the *default* value `socks`

Testing the routes

We need to get back to our phone book example if we want to test our newly created routes. The routes file is compiled and executed when we visit `localhost:9000`.

```
Compilation error

object Entries is not a member of package controllers

In /path/to/play-starter-scala/conf/routes at line 8.

 5  # Home page
 6  GET     /                          controllers.Application.index
 7
 8  GET     /entries                   controllers.Entries.list(filter ?= "")
 9  GET     /entries/new               controllers.Entries.add
10  GET     /entries/:id               controllers.Entries.edit(id: Long)
11  POST    /entries/:id/remove        controllers.Entries.remove(id: Long)
12  POST    /entries                   controllers.Entries.save
13
```

Play provides us with a hint that the **Entries** controller is missing. So, we will implement it next.

Handling HTTP requests by controller actions

A `controller` is a subclass of the `Controller` class. It consists of a set of (generally static) methods that process an HTTP request by computing an HTTP response and sending it back to the web browser. The controller methods are called *actions*.

The Java API has no special representation of actions. In Scala, an action can be basically seen as a function of the following type:

```
(play.api.mvc.Request => play.api.mvc.Result)
```

Instant Play Framework Starter

The Java classes `Controller`, `Request`, and `Result` that are used in the request-response cycle, are located in the package `play.mvc`. The Scala API is located at `play.api.mvc`.

Providing dummy implementations

Apparently, the routes file has errors because of the missing controller `Entries` (not to be confused with `models.Entries`).

To fix that, we create `app/controllers/Entries.java` with the following content:

```java
package controllers;

import play.mvc.*;

public class Entries extends Controller {
  public static Result list(String filter) {
    return TODO;
  }

  public static Result remove(long id) {
    return TODO;
  }

  public static Result add() {
    return TODO;
  }

  public static Result edit(long id) {
    return TODO;
  }

  public static Result save() {
    return TODO;
  }

}
```

The corresponding Scala code looks almost the same:

```scala
package controllers

import play.api.mvc._

object Entries extends Controller {

  def list(filter: String) = TODO

  def remove(id: Long) = TODO
```

```
    def add = TODO

    def edit(id: Long) = TODO

    def save = TODO
}
```

We actually don't have provided `real` implementations of the controller methods. Instead, we return Play's empty result (Java) and action (Scala) implementation, **TODO**. Now the controller is syntactically correct and can be compiled.

To trigger the routes generator, we are reloading the web pages of our Java and Scala applications. So now, the error should disappear.

Of course we can already test what happens when we visit a specific URL listed in our routes file, say `localhost:9000/entries?filter=test`. According to the route, the controller method `controllers.Entries.list("test")` is called, which returns the **TODO** dummy page:

URL redirection with reverse routes

The router can also be used to programmatically generate an URL. Each controller has a so-called reverse controller in a sub-package `routes` of the corresponding controller class. For example, the controller `controllers.Entries` has a reverse controller `controllers.routes.Entries`, which contains (almost) the same methods. The difference is that the reverse controller methods return a *Call* instead of a *Result*, where a call corresponds to an URL.

As an example, we will redirect our base URL `localhost:9000` to the list of phone book entries located at `localhost:9000/entries`.

Technically, the Play server performs the redirect by sending an HTTP 302 response to the client, where the response header contains the new URL. In contrast to directly calling the controller method `Entries.list("")`, the browser location is changed.

In Java, we replace the body of the `Application` controller's `index` method with:

```
public class Application extends Controller {

    public static Result index() {
        return redirect(routes.Entries.list(""));
    }

}
```

The Scala solution allows us to omit the argument of the `list` method and use the default method defined in the `routes` definition:

```
object Application extends Controller {

  def index = Action {
    Redirect(routes.Entries.list())
  }

}
```

The `routes` file tells us that a request of `localhost:9000/` invokes `Application.index`, which in turn invokes `Entries.list` with a redirect to `localhost:9000/entries`.

We will also use reverse controllers to generate links in our view templates. We have all our URI patterns centralized in the routes file. Using reverse controllers instead of hard-coded links provides us with the certainty that all links are correct—which is one of the several advantages of using Play.

Implementing controller actions

Now we have met all the requirements to implement our first two controller methods, `list` and `remove`.

The Java code

We edit `app/controllers/Entries.java` and insert the following method bodies. Please note that we will adjust the `index` view template accordingly:

```
public static Result list(String filter) {
  Seq<Entry> entries = models.Entries.findByName(filter);
  return ok(views.html.index.render(entries));
}
```

The `list` method first calls the `findByName` method of our DAO `models.Entries`, which returns all phone book entries where the given `filter` is part of the entry name.

Then the `views.html.index` view template renders the list of phone book entries. The result is an HTML page, which is returned by the action with the HTTP 200 OK status and the correct content type `text/html`. The content type is inferred based on the value passed to the status function (but could be changed by calling `.as(...)`).

The implementation of `remove` looks very similar to that of the `list` method:

```
public static Result remove(long id) {
  models.Entries.delete(id);
  return redirect(routes.Entries.list(""));
}
```

First, the DAO is called to delete the entry by it's ID. Then a redirect to the list of phone book entries is returned.

Because `Entries.findByName` returns a sequence of phone book entries of type `Seq<Entry>`, we additionally need to import the following classes:

```
import scala.collection.Seq;
import models.Entry;
```

The Scala code

We edit `app/controllers/Entries.scala` and insert the implementation of `list`:

```
def list(filter: String) = Action {
  val entries = DAO.findByName(filter.trim)
  Ok(views.html.index(entries))
}
```

The implementation of `remove` is also analogous to Java:

```
def remove(id: Long) = Action {
  DAO.delete(id)
  Redirect(routes.Entries.list())
}
```

Our DAO `models.Entries` has the same name as our current controller. To resolve this name clash, we had to provide the fully-qualified name of the DAO in the Java implementation of the `list` action. In Scala we have the ability to substitute the imported class name with a shortcut by specifying the following import:

```
import models.{Entries => DAO}
```

What comes next

When we reload the page, the compiler complains that the `index` view template currently expects a string instead of a list of entries. We will fix that when implementing our view templates.

Composing the UI from view templates

The views of a Play application are based on a safe template engine. View templates (views) are HTML files with dynamic parts using Scala as an expression language. Compared to other template languages there are no special tags or surrounding blocks for an embedded template syntax. Template expressions begin with the @ character and are simply mixed in to your HTML code.

With the help of Play's template parser, a Scala version of the template is generated. For example, we use this in our controllers. When a view is rendered, the compiled template expressions are evaluated. The occurrence of a template expression is replaced by its value. The result is a static HTML page.

Physically, templates are located in the folder `app/views` or one of its subfolders. After views are compiled they are located in the package `views.html` or one of its sub packages. For example, the fully-qualified name of `app/views/index.scala.html` is `views.html.index`.

Syntax of view templates

The syntax of view templates are basically a combination of HTML for the static parts and Scala for the dynamic parts.

View parameters

The first line of a view is mandatory and declares the template parameters. It starts with an @ character followed by one or more parameter blocks. A parameter block is denoted in parentheses () and contains a comma-separated list of parameter declarations.

Like in Scala, a parameter has a name followed by a colon : and a type. Generic parameter types are denoted with [] instead of <>. For example:

```
@(entries: Seq[models.Entry])
```

View imports

The declaration of view parameters is optionally followed by import declarations. Please remember that the underlying syntax is that of Scala. Use _ instead of * as a wildcard. For example:

```
@import java.util.List
@import views.html.helper._
```

View expressions

Template expressions are Scala expressions, with one exception—a simplified `for` expression. Strictly speaking, the HTML code is also a template expression, as follows:

- `<markup>...</markup>`: It is an HTML code, but contains template expressions

But it is not considered as such in our short overview, as follows:

- `@expression`: It is a simple expression such as `@list.getSize()`
- `@(complex expression)`: It indicates multiple tokens such as `@(e1 + e2)`
- `@{block expression}`: It represents block of expressions such as `@{e1; e2}`
- `@*comment*@`: It indicates a comment, but unlike `<!--comment-->` it is not rendered
- `@@`: It denotes a single `@` character has to be escaped

Additionally, there are the following control structures:

- `@if(condition) {...} else {...}`: This is the if-expression, the `else` part is optional
- `@for(to <- from; ...) {...}`: This is the `for` loop, which returns the evaluated block

Sometimes it may also be helpful to declare the reusable blocks without introducing a new template:

- `@name(param: Type, ...) = {...}`: This declares a function `name`

For a complete list of template expressions, please refer to the Play framework documentation.

Composing view templates

A view can be seen as a function. It computes an HTML fragment based on specific parameters. In that manner, views are reusable building blocks. They are referenced by their fully-qualified name, for example, `@viewName(params){param}{...}`.

Parameters are of an arbitrary Java or Scala type. Especially, blocks of HTML can be passed to views. The type of an HTML block is `play.api.templates.Html` for both Java and Scala.

When a view is called, it is evaluated. This is done by evaluating all of its contained template expressions and subsequently concatenating the results. The result is of type `play.api.templates.Html`.

Example

A new Play application has two views, `main` and `index`. The `index` view calls the `main` view, passing the required parameters. In general, templates are called to have the same content on all the pages of a website:

```
@(message: String)
@main("Sample") {
  <h1>@message</h1>
}
```

The `main` view takes two parameters, which are used as simple template expressions:

```
@(title: String)(content: Html)
<html>
  <head>
    <title>@title</title>
  </head>
  <body>
    @content
  </body>
</html>
```

Visiting the base URL calls the `Application.index` action, which renders the `index` view.

The fact that functions such as the `main` view can have multiple parameter blocks is new to programmers. This allows us to denote a multi-line block using `{}` instead of `()` if there is only one parameter.

Nesting view templates

The `main` template is a reusable building block, which is used within the `index` template. The `index` view renders some HTML code and passes it as parameter to the `main` view. In general, the most specific parts of a page are rendered first and passed as an argument to more general and reusable building blocks (such as a menu bar) of a web page.

Implementing the phone book views

Let's get started with implementing the views of our phone book sample.

Prerequisites

We use the CSS framework Twitter Bootstrap to style our application. These styles are annotated in `class="..."` attributes of the HTML elements. The styles are not explained in detail here because they do not affect the functionality of the phone book application.

To install Twitter Bootstrap, please download it at `http://twitter.github.com/bootstrap/` and extract its contents to the `public/` folder of our Java and Scala application. The result should look similar to this:

/path/to/play-starter-scala/public

```
└─bootstrap
|   └─css
|   └─img
|   └─js
└─images
└─javascripts
└─stylesheets
```

The index view template

Currently, the compiler complains about the wrong parameter type of the `index` view located at `app/views/index.scala.html`. We fix that by introducing the `entries` parameter of type `Seq[Entry]`. Also we replace the content passed to the `main` view:

```
@(entries: Seq[Entry])

@main {

  <form action="@routes.Entries.list()" method="GET">
    <div class="input-append">
      <input type="text" name="filter" class="input-xxlarge"
             autofocus="">
      <button type="submit" class="btn">Search</button>
    </div>
  </form>

  <a href="@routes.Entries.add()"
     class="btn btn-small btn-primary">New entry</a>

  @list(entries)

}
```

The `main` view does not take the title parameter any more. We replaced the welcome message of the initial view with the following:

* `<form>…</form>`: This is an input field to search phone book entries
* `<a>…</a>`: This is a link to add new phone book entries, displayed as a button
* `@list(entries)`: This is a list of current phone book entries

As we already stated, we use reverse controllers instead of hard-coded URLs.

The HTTP method of the form is `GET` and it is used in order to append the form data to the request query string. This makes searches bookmarkable.

Instead of `@views.html.list(entries)`, we can write `@list(entries)`. The packages `views.html` and `models` are in scope by default.

The list view template

The list of entries is rendered by a separate view `app/views/list.scala.html`. We create it with the following content for our Java application:

```
@(entries: Seq[Entry])

<table class="table table-hover">
  @for(entry <- entries) {
    <tr>
      <td>
        <strong>@entry.name</strong><br>
        <a href="tel:@entry.phone">@entry.phone</a>
        <form action="@routes.Entries.remove(entry.id)"
            method="POST">
          <a href="@routes.Entries.edit(entry.id)"
             class="btn btn-small">Edit</a>
          <input type="submit" value="Remove" class="btn btn-small">
        </form>
      </td>
    </tr>
  }
</table>
```

Our `Entry` implementations slightly differ in Java and Scala. In Scala, we avoid them to cope with `null` value handling. Instead, we use the generic `Option[T]` type, which has two implementations, `Some[T]` and `None[T]`.

Here we get `Some(id)` if `entry.id` is defined, otherwise, we get `None`. The `Option` type plays well together with the `for` expression. This is our Scala implementation:

```
@(entries: Seq[Entry])

<table class="table table-hover">
  @for(entry <- entries; id <- entry.id) {
    <tr>
      <td>
        <strong>@entry.name</strong><br>
        <a href="tel:@entry.phone">@entry.phone</a>
        <form action="@routes.Entries.remove(id)"
            method="POST">
          <a href="@routes.Entries.edit(id)"
             class="btn btn-small">Edit</a>
```

```
            <input type="submit" value="Remove" class="btn btn-small">
          </form>
        </td>
      </tr>
    }
</table>
```

According to the call of the `list` view in the `index` view, there is one parameter `entries` of type `Seq[Entry]`. The phonebook entries are aligned in a table by iterating the given sequence and producing a table row for each `Entry`.

In Scala we do not expect `None` values here. Anyway, if `entry.id` is `None`, no table row is generated for that entry.

A table row consists of the phone book entry name, the phone number, and two buttons for editing and removing phone book entries. The phone number is displayed as a click-to-call link for mobile browsers. We use the reverse controllers for linking our `edit` and `remove` actions.

The main view template

Finally, we have to provide a proper implementation of the `main` view:

```
@(content: Html)

@style(asset: String) = {
  <link rel="stylesheet" href="@routes.Assets.at(asset)">
}

<!DOCTYPE html>
<html>
  <head>
    <title>Play Framework Starter Guide</title>
    @style("bootstrap/css/bootstrap.css")
    @style("bootstrap/css/bootstrap-responsive.css")
    @style("stylesheets/main.css")
  </head>
  <body>
    <div class="navbar navbar-inverse navbar-fixed-top">
      <div class="navbar-inner">
        <div class="container">
          <a class="brand" href="/">Phonebook</a>
        </div>
      </div>
    </div>
    <div class="container">
      @content
    </div>
  </body>
</html>
```

We removed the `title` parameter of the initial `main` view implementation and declared the `style` function, which we use in the HTML `head` element to include our CSS stylesheets.

The body consists of the popular Twitter Bootstrap `navbar`, which displays our brand, Phonebook, and the `content` argument of the `main` view.

Fine-tuning the CSS style

We have to customize the Twitter Bootstrap style for our design. Please replace the content of `public/stylesheets/main.css` with the following:

```css
@media (min-width:979px) {
  body           { padding-top:60px }
}
form             { margin:0 }
table            { margin-top:8px }
td               { position:relative }
td > form        { position:absolute; right:8px; top:14px }
```

We ensure correct alignment to the top of big screens. The margin of tables and forms is also tweaked a little bit. Also, we align our Entry buttons to the right-hand side of a table row.

Now reload our page. This is what it looks like:

Providing some test data

Unfortunately, our data store is empty and we are currently unable to add entries. Nevertheless, to test the functionality we need to add some test data.

One easy way to achieve this is to intercept the application start-up and create some test data by implementing `app/Global.java` in the Java project:

```java
import models.*;
import play.*;

public class Global extends GlobalSettings {
  @Override
  public void onStart(Application app) {
    Entries.save(newEntry("Guillaume Bort",
        "+33 5 55 55 55 55"));
    Entries.save(newEntry("Sadek Drobi", "+33 5 55 55 55 55"));
  }
```

```java
    private Entry newEntry(String name, String phone) {
      Entry entry = new Entry();
      entry.name = name;
      entry.phone = phone;
      return entry;
    }
  }
```

The `onStart` method is called by Play on the application startup. So we have the opportunity to initialize our data store by programmatically saving phone book entries.

For the Scala project, we create `app/Global.scala`:

```scala
import models.{Entry, Entries => DAO}
import play.api._

object Global extends GlobalSettings {

  override def onStart(app: Application) {

    DAO.save(Entry("Guillaume Bort", "+33 5 55 55 55 55"))
    DAO.save(Entry("Sadek Drobi", "+33 5 55 55 55 55"))

  }
}
```

Feel free to play around with our first version of the phone book prototype!

2 – Dealing with user input

There are two buttons displayed on our main page that currently have no implementation on the backend side, namely **New entry** and **Edit**. Our next goal is to implement these by creating a user interface for adding new phone book entries and for editing existing ones. The functionality of the **Remove** button on the search result page will be implemented later.

Defining a form

It is straightforward to add new functionality to our application. We need to implement two things, the HTML form with the input fields for a phone book entry and a corresponding form abstraction on the server side. We start with the server side.

The server side

Users submit HTML form fields on the client side. The data is sent as text to the server packaged within an HTTP request. It has to be parsed on the server side. A corresponding typed data structure is filled with the form field values.

Instant Play Framework Starter

Binding data with a Java form

Data binding is a common task in the world of web programming. Play provides an easy to use vehicle for this, simply called *Form*.

We need to add two standard imports to our `Entries` controller before we can define a Form:

```
import play.data.Form;
import static play.data.Form.form;
```

Given that, we declare the Form the following way. The existing code of our file is unaffected:

```
public class Entries extends Controller {

  final static Form<Entry> entryForm = form(Entry.class);

  // ...
}
```

We wrapped the `Entry` type in a `Form` instance, which we use in our controller to bind the data from a request in the `save` method:

```
public static Result save() {
  Entry entry = entryForm.bindFromRequest(request()).get();
  models.Entries.save(entry);
  return redirect(routes.Entries.list(""));
}
```

After persisting the entity, we redirect to the phone entry list.

The `add` method is also implemented:

```
public static Result add() {
  Form<Entry> form = entryForm.fill(new Entry());
  return ok(views.html.edit.render(form, "Add entry"));
}
```

Because a new entry has no initial data, we fill our form with an empty `Entry` and call the `edit` view. The same view will be used to render the existing phone book entries, so we send the form data along with an appropriate label reflecting the current action.

Finally, we need to implement the `edit` method:

```
public static Result edit(long id) {
  Entry entry = models.Entries.findById(id);
  if (entry != null) {
    Form<Entry> form = entryForm.fill(entry);
    return ok(views.html.edit.render(form, "Edit entry"));
```

```
    } else {
      return redirect(routes.Entries.list(""));
    }
  }
```

Here we render an existing phone book entry. Because we don't know if another user changed or removed our entry in the meanwhile, we load the current entry from our storage by its ID. If no entry is found, we will return to the list of entries.

Binding data with a Scala form

Play for Scala provides a different API for dealing with user input. To use it, we have to add some imports to our `Entries` controller:

```
import models.{Entry, Entries => DAO}
import play.api.data._
import play.api.data.Forms._
```

Then we define the form:

```
object Entries extends Controller {

  val entryForm = Form(
    mapping(
      "name" -> text,
      "phone" -> text,
      "id" -> optional(longNumber)
    )(Entry.apply)(Entry.unapply))

  // ...

}
```

A form is constructed with a mapping of field names to field parsers, where a field parser is technically also a type of mapping. This allows us to easily define nested structures.

There are two types of mappings: **composite mappings** and **value mappings**. Simply put, composite mappings are a hint to the form parser on how to look for nested input fields. Value mappings provide the parser with information, including which type of data it has to deal with; for example, text or numeric fields.

Finally, we have to specify how objects are created from parsed form data and vice versa. The parsed data is a tuple. In our example, we use the `apply` and `unapply` methods of our case class `Entry`. The `apply` method takes a tuple and `unapply` results in a tuple.

Instant Play Framework Starter

To bind the `Entry` from the request in our `save` method, we have to bring the request into scope. The easiest way to do this is by using the `implicit` keyword:

```
def save = Action { implicit request =>
  val entry = entryForm.bindFromRequest.get
  DAO.save(entry)
  Redirect(routes.Entries.list())
}
```

Adding phone book entries looks almost the same as in Java:

```
def add = Action {
  val form = entryForm.fill(Entry())
  Ok(views.html.edit(form, "Add entry"))
}
```

The difference with `edit` between Java and Scala is that `findById` returns an `Option[Entry]`. Again, this means that we don't have to cope with the `null` values.

```
def edit(id: Long) = Action {
  DAO.findById(id) map { entry =>
    val form = entryForm.fill(entry)
    Ok(views.html.edit(form, "Edit entry"))
  } getOrElse {
    Redirect(routes.Entries.list())
  }
}
```

If the finder returns `Some(Entry)`, the edit form is displayed. Otherwise, it returns `None` and we redirect to the list of phone book entries.

The client side

The edit page displayed on the client side is created by rendering the `edit` view template. Create `app/views/edit.scala.html` with the following content:

```
@(entryForm: Form[Entry], heading: String)

@main {

  <h1>@heading</h1>

  <form action="@routes.Entries.save()" method="POST">
    <input type="hidden" name="id" value="@entryForm("id").value">
    <div>
      <label for="name">Name</label>
      <div class="input">
        <input type="text" id="name" name="name"
```

```
            value="@entryForm("name").value" autofocus="">
      </div>
    </div>
    <div>
      <label for="phone">Phone</label>
      <div class="input">
        <input type="text" id="phone" name="phone"
            value="@entryForm("phone").value">
      </div>
    </div>
    <div>
      <button type="submit" class="btn btn-primary">Save</button>
      <a class="btn" href="@routes.Entries.list()">Cancel</a>
    </div>
  </form>
}
```

The HTML form consists of one hidden input field containing the ID of the entry. The ID is needed on the server side to identify the entity to be saved to the data storage.

Furthermore, there are two input fields holding the name and the phone number of our entry. All fields are initialized with the corresponding form value of the given `entryForm` parameter, for example, `@entryForm("name").value`.

On form submission, the reverse controller method `Entries.save` is called. Additionally there is a *cancel* link, which loads the list of phone book entries.

Now we are able to create and edit phone book entries.

Validating user input

It is necessary that we validate the user input before saving it to the data storage. Play does provide an elegant API for that. In Java, we annotate our entity fields with constraints or define a `validate` method for more complex situations. In Scala we already used constraints without mentioning it explicitly.

Play's validation mechanism is built around the Form API and it is therefore executed on the server side. The client submits the form data to the server, where it is bound from the request. If validation constraints are defined, the form validation is triggered. We check if validation errors have occurred, and then either send the form including the validation errors back to the client or go ahead and process the form data.

The server side

On the server side, we have two tasks regarding validation, including attribution of our form fields with constraints, and adapting the control flow of the `save` method.

Instant Play Framework Starter

Defining constraints in Java

The Java API allows us to annotate our constraints directly at the fields of our `Entry` entity. The constraints are statically imported, as shown in the following:

```
package models;

import static play.data.validation.Constraints.*;

public class Entry {

  public Long id;

  @Required
  @MinLength(value = 2)
  public String name;

  @Required
  @Pattern(
    value = "\\+?[0-9\\s]+",
    message = "Optional +, followed by digits & spaces"
  )
  public String phone;

  public Entry() {}

}
```

We marked the fields `name` and `phone` as required. Additionally, the `name` field has to have a minimum length of two characters. Because we use the `tel:` URL scheme to enable click-to-dial links on mobile devices, we have to ensure that phone numbers have the right format.

There is actually no pre-defined constraint checking the validity of phone numbers. In this case, it is sufficient to implement our own constraint using the `Pattern` annotation. This has two arguments: a regular expression and an error message.

During form validation, it is checked if the regular expression matches the current value of the `phone` field. If it does not match the current value, the message is added to the list of error messages associated with the current form field.

Now that we have constraints defined, we need to adjust the control flow of the `save` method.

```
public static Result save() {
  Form<Entry> form = entryForm.bindFromRequest(request());
  if (form.hasErrors()) {
    return badRequest(
      views.html.edit.render(form, "Correct entry"));
  } else {
```

```
        models.Entries.save(form.get());
        return redirect(routes.Entries.list(""));
    }
}
```

When the form is bound from the request, the validation process is automatically started. If the form has errors, we send it back to the server in order to be corrected by the user. If the form contents are valid, the phone book entry is saved, and we redirect to the phone book list.

Defining constraints in Scala

For Scala, the Play developers took a different approach. The constraints are specified directly at the form fields in our `Entries` controller.

First, we have to import the constraints API:

```
import play.api.data.validation.Constraints._
```

Then we add the constraints to our `form` fields:

```
val entryForm = Form(
  mapping(
    "name" -> nonEmptyText(minLength = 2),
    "phone" -> (nonEmptyText verifying pattern(
      """\+?[0-9\s]+""".r,
      error = "Optional +, followed by digits & spaces")
    ),
    "id" -> optional(longNumber)
  )(Entry.apply)(Entry.unapply))
```

The `nonEmptyText` constraint replaces the `text` constraint. It implies, that the field is required. The argument `minLength` defines the minimum length of the `name` field.

The `phone` field is marked as required. We added the regular expression along with an appropriate error message for verifying phone numbers:

```
def save = Action { implicit request =>
  entryForm.bindFromRequest.fold(
    errors => BadRequest(views.html.edit(errors, "Correct entry")),
    entry => {
      DAO.save(entry)
      Redirect(routes.Entries.list())
    }
  )
}
```

The `fold` method defined in the `Form` class provides us with a convenient syntax for handling form errors and validation success.

The client side

Our program does already compile and run, but we also need to customize the edit view in regards to the way that validation errors are displayed:

```
<form action="@routes.Entries.save()" method="POST">
  <input type="hidden" name="id" value="@entryForm("id").value">
  <div class="control-group
      @if(entryForm("name").hasErrors) {error}">
    <label for="name">Name</label>
    <div class="input">
      <input type="text" id="name" name="name"
          value="@entryForm("name").value" autofocus="">
      <span class="help-inline">@(entryForm("name").errors.map{ e =>
          play.api.i18n.Messages(e.message , e.args: _*)
      }.mkString(", "))</span>
    </div>
  </div>
  <div class="control-group
      @if(entryForm("phone").hasErrors) {error}">
    <label for="phone">Phone</label>
    <div class="input">
      <input type="text" id="phone" name="phone"
          value="@entryForm("phone").value">
      <span class="help-inline">@(entryForm("phone").errors.map{e =>
          play.api.i18n.Messages(e.message , e.args: _*)
      }.mkString(", "))</span>
    </div>
  </div>
  <div>
    <button type="submit" class="btn btn-primary">Save</button>
    <a class="btn" href="@routes.Entries.list()">Cancel</a>
  </div>
</form>
```

> Please note that internationalization (i18n) is not needed here, and that it is going beyond the topic of the book sample. For more information on i18n, please refer to the Play documentation.

This view compiles only in Scala. Because of a small discrepancy between the Java and Scala API, the string `e.args` must be replaced with `e.arguments` in the highlighted lines for the Java version.

We have added some additional error message handling to two visible input fields here, and to be honest, there is so much repetition already that the source code starts to look really horrible. Not to imagine how a more complex form would look like.

But we can do better...

Using form template helpers

We have a powerful template language at our hands that allows us to easily reduce unnecessary repetition. For example, we can define a function, which generates an input field given a specific form field. Play already comes with helpers, which exactly do this-the form template helpers.

We replace our `edit` form with this code, which is the same for Java and Scala:

```
@(entryForm: Form[Entry], heading: String)

@import views.html.helper._
@import views.html.helper.twitterBootstrap._

@main {

  <h1>@heading</h1>

  @form(action=routes.Entries.save()) {

    <input type="hidden" name="id" value="@entryForm("id").value">

    @inputText(
        entryForm("name"),
        '_class -> "control-group",
        '_label -> "Name",
        '_showConstraints -> false,
        'autofocus -> ""
    )

    @inputText(
        entryForm("phone"),
        '_class -> "control-group",
        '_label -> "Phone",
        '_showConstraints -> false
    )
```

```
      <div>
        <button type="submit" class="btn btn-primary">Save</button>
        <a class="btn" href="@routes.Entries.list()">Cancel</a>
      </div>

   }

}
```

First, the helpers are imported; we especially need the Twitter Bootstrap support here, to automatically apply the right style. Please note that the Twitter Bootstrap imports contain a `FieldConstructor` implementation, which defines how to render a form field and which is implicitly used by all default Play view helpers, such as `@form` and `@inputText`.

We replaced the `<form>` element with `@form`. It is no longer necessary to specify the HTTP method, because the reverse controller we use already contains this information.

Next, we replaced all the elements around our visible input fields with `@inputText`. This template has three different kinds of arguments. First, we specified the `form` field, followed by special arguments of `@inputText` (starting with `'_`), and then followed at the end by a list of HTML attributes, which will be appended to the generated HTML input element.

The CSS style `control-group` has to be set, because the current Twitter Bootstrap support of Play is a little bit outdated.

The imported helper `twitterBootstrapFieldConstructor.scala.html` contains the HTML code of a Twitter Bootstrap `form` field. This code can be compared with one of the Twitter Bootstrap form samples to get more details about the completeness of the helper implementation.

The `'_label` argument contains the visible label of the input field. Finally, we set `'_showConstraints` to `false` because we don't want our field constraints to be displayed.

3 – Connecting to a database

In this last part of the book, we are going to replace our self-implemented data store with a real database.

To ease database related development, Play has a built-in support for two database access layers, namely Ebean for Java and Anorm for Scala. In the near future, a third candidate will be bundled with Play; Slick for Scala. They all use JDBC under the hood and provide us with nice APIs to close the gap between our application code and the underlying database.

Accessing data with Ebean for Java

Ebean is an object-relational mapper for Java, based on an internal **domain-specific language** (**DSL**) for querying the database. That means native SQL statements are created automatically when executing queries.

Customizing the configuration

By default, a new Play application for Java that has been created with the `play new` command has all the required dependencies pre-defined in our SBT project definition `project/Build.scala`:

```
val appDependencies = Seq(
  javaCore,
  javaJdbc,
  javaEbean
)
```

We register the H2 in-memory JDBC driver for our database named `default` by uncommenting these two lines in our configuration file `conf/application.conf`:

```
db.default.driver=org.h2.Driver
db.default.url="jdbc:h2:mem:play"
```

To activate the Ebean initialization on application startup, we have to uncomment the following line:

```
ebean.default="models.*"
```

With this property, we specify where to search for *entities*; in our case the class `Entry.java`. Also we define which Ebean server is used to access our entities, in this case *default*, which corresponds to the connection properties previously given.

Now the configuration of Ebean is complete.

Creating the database schema

We have two choices when it comes to creating a database schema; we either do it manually or automatically. Ebean supports automatic DDL generation, that is, it produces SQL scripts based on our entities. This is good for testing or as a starting point for large databases, but it is discouraged for production quality applications.

Here we are going to create the database schema manually. Play supports us in tracking and executing our database changes. We call these changes *evolutions*; they are divided into files located in `conf/evolutions/<database-name>/`. In our case `<database-name>` is `default`. The first evolution has the name `1.sql`, the second `2.sql`, and so on. These files contain the so-called *up* and *down* scripts, which are used to *change* and *revert* the database. A revert may occur during development if an existing evolution changes.

Instant Play Framework Starter

So let's create our first database evolution. As mentioned previously, it is located in `conf/evolutions/default/1.sql` with the following content:

```
# --- !Ups

create table entry (
  id                  bigint not null,
  name                varchar(255) not null,
  phone               varchar(255) not null,
  constraint pk_entry primary key (id))
;

create sequence entry_seq start with 1;

# --- !Downs

drop table if exists entry;

drop sequence if exists seq_entry;
```

The `Ups` and the `Downs` comments are mandatory. In the `Ups` part we create a table entry; rows of phone book entries with a unique ID, a name, and a phone number. Additionally, we are using a sequence to generate our unique IDs. In the `Downs` part we specify how to revert the changes, which in our case is simply by dropping the table and the sequence.

Before we start our application and create the schema, we have to implement our Ebean based model.

Implementing the model

Ebean uses the same mapping annotations as the Java Persistence API (JPA). These are located in the package `javax.persistence`. We use the `@Entity` annotation that denotes that our `Entry` class is mapped to a table with the same name. The `@Id` annotation marks our Primary key field.

We implement `app/models/Entry.java` as follows:

```
package models;

import play.db.ebean.Model;

import javax.persistence.Entity;
import javax.persistence.Id;

import static play.data.validation.Constraints.*;

@Entity
public class Entry extends Model {
```

```
    @Id
    public Long id;

    @Required
    @MinLength(value = 2)
    public String name;

    @Required
    @Pattern(
      value = "\\+?[0-9\\s]+",
      message = "Optional +, followed by digits & spaces"
    )
    public String phone;

    public Entry() {}

    public static Finder<Long,Entry> find =
        new Finder<Long,Entry>(Long.class, Entry.class);
}
```

Ebean has a default naming convention that maps Java names written in camel-case `fooBarBaz` to database names in snake-case format `foo_bar_baz`. Of course this convention can be customized.

We extend the `Model` class, which is part of the Play Framework. It contains convenient methods and a `Finder` class that we use to create a finder for our `Entry` entity.

Next, we are using the query DSL of Ebean to implement our DAO methods. Please modify `app/models/Entries.java` accordingly:

```
package models;

import static play.libs.Scala.toSeq;
import scala.collection.Seq;

public class Entries {
  public static void delete(long id) {
        Entry.find.ref(id).delete();
  }
  public static Entry findById(long id) {
    return Entry.find.byId(id);
  }
  public static Seq<Entry> findByName(String filter) {
        return toSeq(Entry.find
          .where()
```

```
            .ilike("name", "%"+filter+"%")
            .findList());
    }
    public static void save(Entry entry) {
        if (entry.id == null) {
            entry.save();
        } else {
            entry.update();
        }
    }
}
```

As you can see, it is pretty straightforward to query the database with Ebean.

- `delete`: This uses the `Finder` of `Entry` to delete an entity referenced by its ID.
- `findById`: This uses the `Finder` of `Entry` to find an entity by its ID.
- `findByName`: This finds all entities matching a specific criteria. We use `ilike` to find case insensitive matches of a given filter within the column `name`.
- `save`: This persists an entity. If it is new, the ID is generated by our database sequence and automatically set by Ebean in our `model` class; else all fields of the associated database row are updated.

Ebean, by default, executes a query in an implicit transaction, so we don't have to care here about session and transaction management.

Running the application

We can now start reloading our application in the browser:

```
Database 'default' needs evolution!
An SQL script will be run on your database -  Apply this script now!
This SQL script must be run:
1 # --- Rev:1,Ups - 7e78633
2 create table entry (
3   id                        bigint not null,
4   name                      varchar(255) not null,
5   phone                     varchar(255) not null,
6   constraint pk_entry primary key (id))
7 ;
```

Play checks on each page reload in development mode to see if database evolutions have changed. If there are new evolutions or an existing one has changed, Play asks to apply the scripts. We press the **Apply this script now!** button to execute the `Ups` sections of the changed scripts in the right-hand side order.

Now we have a working Ebean implementation of our model.

Accessing data with Anorm for Scala

Anorm for Scala takes a different approach than Ebean for Java. Queries are written in SQL, because Anorm assumes that SQL is already the best DSL to access a database. There is no need for an Object Relational Mapper. Scala has all the features needed to transform the JDBC data into Scala structures.

Customizing the configuration

When creating a new Play application for Scala with the `play new` command, the required dependencies `jdbc` and `anorm` are already configured in the SBT build definition file `project/Build.scala`:

```
val appDependencies = Seq(
  jdbc,
  anorm
)
```

Like for our Ebean example, we enable the in-memory H2 database in `conf/application.conf` by uncommenting the following lines:

```
db.default.driver=org.h2.Driver
db.default.url="jdbc:h2:mem:play"
```

There is no additional configuration needed.

Creating the database schema

Again we will create the database DDL script `conf/evolutions/default/1.sql`.

```
# --- !Ups

create table entry (
  id                        bigint auto_increment primary key,
  name                      varchar(255) not null,
  phone                     varchar(255) not null)
;

# --- !Downs

drop table if exists entry;
```

We declare our primary key column as `auto_increment` to automatically generate IDs in the database when inserting new phone book entries. Ebean needs a database sequence for ID generation, but Anorm also works well with an auto increment key.

Implementing the model

The database access is implementation in the DAO through `models/Entries.scala`. Our entity `case class Entry` remains unchanged.

The necessary imports for using Anorm and JDBC connections are also added:

```
package models

import anorm._
import anorm.SqlParser._
import play.api.Play.current
import play.api.db.DB

case class Entry(name: String = "", phone: String = "",
    id: Option[Long] = None)

object Entries {

  val simple = {
    get[String]("entry.name") ~
    get[String]("entry.phone") ~
    get[Option[Long]]("entry.id") map {
      case name ~ phone ~ id => Entry(name, phone, id)
    }
  }

  def delete(id: Long) = DB.withConnection {
    implicit connection =>
      SQL("delete from entry where id = {id}")
        .on('id -> id)
        .executeUpdate()
  }

  def findById(id: Long) = DB.withConnection {
    implicit connection =>
      SQL("select * from entry where id = {id}")
        .on('id -> id)
        .singleOpt(simple)
  }

  def findByName(filter: String) = DB.withConnection {
    implicit connection =>
      SQL("select * from entry where lower(name) like {filter}")
```

```
            .on('filter -> ("%"+filter.toLowerCase+"%"))
            .as(simple.*)
    }

    def save(entry: Entry) = DB.withConnection {
      implicit connection =>
        if (entry.id.isDefined) {
          SQL("""update entry set name={name}, phone={phone}
                 where id = {id}""")
            .on('name -> entry.name, 'phone -> entry.phone,
                'id -> entry.id)
            .executeUpdate()
        } else {
          SQL("""insert into Entry(name, phone)
                 values ({name}, {phone})""")
            .on('name -> entry.name, 'phone -> entry.phone)
            .executeInsert()
        }
    }
}
```

The *row parser* `simple` defines how rows of our database table `Entry` are retrieved. For each column, we specify the type and the name, for example, `get[String]("entry.name")`. These definitions are concatenated with the tilde character `~`. Finally, we tell Anorm how to create an `Entry` object of a given row.

Unlike Ebean, we have to explicitly retrieve a new database connection when we execute database queries. We do this by calling `DB.withConnection`. The Anorm SQL API needs an implicit connection to be in scope.

With the connection in place, we are able to implement our database queries based on plain SQL. In Anorm, we start a query by passing our SQL statement to the `SQL` method, which returns an `SqlQuery` object. Placeholders for variable values are denoted within curly braces `{}`. On the `SqlQuery` object, we call the `on()` method to specify the placeholder values. Finally we execute the query.

Anorm provides us with different methods for querying the database. Here we use:

- `executeUpdate`: This is used to execute a SQL `update` or `delete` statement.
- `executeInsert`: This is used to execute a SQL `insert` statement.
- `singleOpt(simple)`: This is used to execute a SQL `select` statement and retrieve an optional single result, returned as a Scala `Option` type. We specify our row parser `simple` to tell Anorm how to retrieve rows.

- `as(simple.*)`: This is used to execute a SQL select statement and retrieve a list of result rows. Again, we specify our row parser and call the `*` method to apply it to all the result rows.

Running the application

When running our application, we are asked to apply the new database evolution. We do so by pressing the **Apply this script now!** button.

Accessing data with Slick for Scala

Slick increases the degree of scalability and type-safety by allowing us to write database queries natively in Scala. Instead of writing SQL, we use an API that is very similar to that of Scala collections. Under the hood, Slick features a query compiler, which produces the SQL code for the underlying database.

Customizing the configuration

As of Play 2.1, we have to add an external dependency to the SBT build definition `project/Build.scala` in order to use Slick:

```
val appDependencies = Seq(
  jdbc,
  "com.typesafe.slick" %% "slick" % "1.0.0"
)
```

The `jdbc` module is also needed; the `anorm` module can be removed.

Don't forget to regenerate your project files via `play idea` or `play eclipse` to update your class path accordingly if you use one of these IDEs.

Again we enable the in-memory H2 database in `conf/application.conf`.

```
db.default.driver=org.h2.Driver
db.default.url="jdbc:h2:mem:play"
```

Implementing the model

As mentioned previously, Slick has a query compiler that generates SQL statements. We give Slick a hint about which SQL dialect to use by importing an appropriate `Driver` and `ExtendedProfile` respectively (replaced by `JdbcDriver` with Slick 1.1).

Please create the file `app/models/DAL.scala` with the following content:

```
package models

trait Profile {
```

```
    val driver: slick.driver.ExtendedProfile
    val db: scala.slick.session.Database

}
```

The `driver` variable holds the specific Slick database driver. We also need to add a variable `db`, which is used to create database sessions and transactions.

The data access object

We wrap our `Entries` **data access object** (**DAO**) in the `EntriesComponent` trait and use the self-type mechanism to inject the profile properties into our component. Afterwards, the driver objects are imported.

This is the content of `app/models/Entries.scala`:

```
package models

case class Entry(name: String = "", phone: String = "",
    id: Option[Long] = None)

trait EntriesComponent { self: Profile =>

  import driver.simple._
  import Database.threadLocalSession

  object Entries extends Table[Entry]("ENTRY") {
    def id = column[Long]("ID", O.PrimaryKey, O.AutoInc)
    def name = column[String]("NAME")
    def phone = column[String]("PHONE")
    def * = name ~ phone ~ id.? <> (Entry, Entry.unapply _)

    def delete(id: Long) = db withSession {
      Query(this).where(_.id is id).delete
    }

    def findById(id: Long) = db withSession {
      Query(this).where(_.id is id).firstOption
    }

    def findByName(filter: String) = db withSession {
      val search = "%"+filter.toLowerCase+"%"
      Query(this).where(_.name.toLowerCase like search).list
    }

    def save(entry: Entry) = db withSession {
      entry.id.fold {
        this.insert(entry)
```

```
      }{ id =>
        Query(this).where(_.id is id).update(entry)
      }
    }
  }
}
```

Similar to Anorm, we provide a mapping between objects and table rows. In particular, we define the type and name of each column along with additional attributes such as primary key and auto increment.

The * method, the so-called "star-projection", is analog to the row parser of Anorm.

Queries are in the so-called "lifted" state, which means that no SQL has been executed so far. We finally do this by calling:

- `delete`: This deletes a specific phone book entry
- `firstOption`: This returns `Option[Entry]`, which may be `None` if no entry with the given ID exists
- `list`: This returns phone book entries that contain a specific name
- `update`: This updates a specific phone book entry

We insert new entities into the database by calling `insert` on the `Entries` object.

The `threadLocalSession` import attaches a database session to the local thread. This session is automatically available for queries.

The data access layer

We will now choose to add the concrete Slick driver binding to our existing **data access layer** (**DAL**) `models/DAL.scala`.

```
import play.api.Play.current
import play.api.db.DB
import scala.slick.session.Database

object DAL extends EntriesComponent
    /* with OtherComponent */ with Profile {
  val driver = scala.slick.driver.H2Driver
  val db = Database.forDataSource(DB.getDataSource("default"))
  val ddl = Entries.ddl // ++ Other.ddl
}
```

All values of the `Profile` trait are defined here. We use `H2Driver` of Slick and the `default` JDBC configuration found in `application.conf` to retrieve a JDBC `DataSource` value.

To prepare the automatic database schema generation, we additionally define the `ddl` value containing the DDL script of our `Entries` table.

The `Entries` DAO is now part of our DAL. Therefore we have to adjust the imports section of our controller `app/controllers/Entries.scala`:

```
import models.Entry
import models.DAL.{Entries => DAO}
```

Generating the database schema

You should remember that we have inserted some test data on startup in our `GlobalSettings` implementation. This is the right place to create our database on application startup.

```
import models.{DAL, Entry}, DAL._, DAL.driver.simple._
import play.api._

object Global extends GlobalSettings {

  override def onStart(app: Application) {

    DAL.db withSession { implicit s: Session =>
      ddl.create
    }

    Entries.save(Entry("Guillaume Bort", "+33 5 55 55 55 55"))
    Entries.save(Entry("Sadek Drobi", "+33 5 55 55 55 55"))

  }

}
```

We use our DAL to bring a session into scope and create our database schema.

You can now run this application.

Now go ahead and start to implement amazing web applications with Play!

Instant Play Framework Starter

People and places you should get to know

If you need help with Play, here are some people and places that will prove invaluable:

Official sites

- Homepage: http://www.playframework.com
- Manual and documentation: http://www.playframework.com/documentation
- Source code: http://github.com/playframework/play20

Articles and tutorials

- *Scoop.it!* is an online magazine for Play. Find an up-to-date collection of articles and tutorials at http://www.scoop.it/t/playframework.
- Don't miss this great resource on Play-related video tutorials at http://yobriefcasts.tv.
- James Ward gives a complete example on how to develop a Play application and how to host it in the cloud at http://www.jamesward.com/2012/05/08/play-2-java-tutorial.
- Listen to a podcast on Play by James Roper, committer to the Play Framework, at http://scalatypes.com/episode-29-james-roper-on-play-2.
- For a tutorial on how to set up a recent IntelliJ IDEA version with Play, go to http://blogs.jetbrains.com/idea/2012/12/getting-started-with-play-20-in-intellij-idea-12.

Community

- Official mailing list: https://groups.google.com/forum/#!forum/play-framework
- Official forums: https://plus.google.com/+playframework
- Unofficial forums: https://plus.google.com/u/0/communities/116192785110716864793
- Official IRC channel: irc://irc.freenode.net:6667/playframework
- User FAQ: http://stackoverflow.com/questions/tagged/playframework

Blogs

- James Ward is a Teacher of the Typesafe Stack and offers many useful pieces of information and tutorials on Play: http://www.jamesward.com
- James Roper is a committer to the Play Framework: http://jazzy.id.au/default/
- A great and more involved blog on Play and Scala: http://mandubian.com
- The blog of Daniel Dietrich, the author of this book: http://danieldietrich.net

Twitter

- Official information about the Play Framework: @playframework
- Guillaume Bort, creator of the Play Framework: @guillaumebort
- Sadek Drobi, co-creator of Play2: @Sadache
- Follow Daniel Dietrich, author of this book: @danieldietrich
- For more open source information, follow Packt at @packtopensource

[PACKT] Thank you for buying
Instant Play Framework Starter

About Packt Publishing

Packt, pronounced 'packed', published its first book "*Mastering phpMyAdmin for Effective MySQL Management*" in April 2004 and subsequently continued to specialize in publishing highly focused books on specific technologies and solutions.

Our books and publications share the experiences of your fellow IT professionals in adapting and customizing today's systems, applications, and frameworks. Our solution based books give you the knowledge and power to customize the software and technologies you're using to get the job done. Packt books are more specific and less general than the IT books you have seen in the past. Our unique business model allows us to bring you more focused information, giving you more of what you need to know, and less of what you don't.

Packt is a modern, yet unique publishing company, which focuses on producing quality, cutting-edge books for communities of developers, administrators, and newbies alike. For more information, please visit our website: `www.packtpub.com`.

Writing for Packt

We welcome all inquiries from people who are interested in authoring. Book proposals should be sent to `author@packtpub.com`. If your book idea is still at an early stage and you would like to discuss it first before writing a formal book proposal, contact us; one of our commissioning editors will get in touch with you.

We're not just looking for published authors; if you have strong technical skills but no writing experience, our experienced editors can help you develop a writing career, or simply get some additional reward for your expertise.

Play Framework Cookbook

ISBN: 978-1-84951-552-8   Paperback: 292 pages

Over 60 incredibly effective recipes to take you under the hood and leverage advanced concepts of the Play framework

1. Make your application more modular, by introducing you to the world of modules.
2. Keep your application up and running in production mode, from setup to monitoring it appropriately.
3. Integrate play applications into your CI environment
4. Keep performance high by using caching

Learning Play! Framework 2

ISBN: 978-1-78216-012-0   Paperback: 290 pages

Start devekoping awesome web applications with this friendly, practical guide to the Play! Framework

1. While driving in Java, tasks are also presented in Scala – a great way to be introduced to this amazing language
2. Create a fully-fledged, collaborative web application – starting from ground zero; all layers are presented in a pragmatic way
3. Gain the advantages associated with developing a fully integrated web framework

Please check **www.PacktPub.com** for information on our titles

[PACKT] PUBLISHING

Akka Essentials

ISBN: 978-1-84951-828-4   Paperback: 334 pages

A practical, step-by-step guide to learn and build Akka's actor-based, distributed, concurrent, and scalable Java applications

1. Build large, distributed, concurrent, and scalable applications using the Akka's Actor model
2. Simple and clear analogy to Java/JEE application development world to explain the concepts
3. Each chapter will teach you a concept by explaining it with clear and lucid examples– each chapter can be read independently

Ext JS 4 Web Application Development Cookbook

ISBN: 978-1-84951-686-0   Paperback: 488 pages

Over 110 easy-to-follow recipes backed up with real-life examples, walking you through basic Ext JS features to advanced application design using Sencha's Ext JS

1. Learn how to build Rich Internet Applications with the latest version of the Ext JS framework in a cookbook style
2. From creating forms to theming your interface, you will learn the building blocks for developing the perfect web application
3. Easy to follow recipes step through practical and detailed examples which are all fully backed up with code, illustrations, and tips

Please check **www.PacktPub.com** for information on our titles

CPSIA information can be obtained
at www.ICGtesting.com
Printed in the USA
LVHW01s0754050618
579621LV00009B/363/P

9 781782 162902